INTRODUCTION

In Search of the "Catholic Vote"
By Frances Kissling

Early in the 1996 electoral game, tacticians identified the Catholic vote as essential to a win at the presidential level. Ralph Reed said it most memorably when he called the Catholic vote "the jump ball of American politics. Whoever comes down with that ball usually wins in November."

Many players vie for the prize. Both major presidential candidates have openly courted the Catholic vote: Bob Dole speaking to the Catholic Press Association, meeting privately with Cardinal Anthony Bevilacqua, chatting cozily with Cardinal John O'Connor; Bill Clinton, careful throughout his presidency to maintain cordial relationships with church leaders (in a decidedly lopsided effort at friendship), staging a photo op with Mother Teresa, hosting editors of Catholic newspapers in the White House.

The candidates are not alone in their quest. Varied public interest groups aim to "educate"—and claim to speak for—Catholics. Late last year, Ralph Reed's Christian Coalition formed an auxiliary called the Catholic Alliance which it hoped would distribute forty million Christian Coalition voter guides in Catholic churches. Another conservative group, the Catholic Campaign for America, entered the fray with plans for massive circulation of a guide to Catholics' opinions on policy issues.

Frances Kissling is president of Catholics for a Free Choice

But no group has been more active than the bishops, the three-hundred-odd putative leaders of the nation's sixty million Catholics. The most visible manifestation of Catholicism in the political arena, the bishops are best known there for their opposition to legal abortion. In every presidential contest since the 1973 *Roe v. Wade* decision, as political scientist Timothy Byrnes observes, the bishops have worked to put abortion at the front and center in electoral campaigns (see page 11).

Most notably, in the wake of the Supreme Court's *Webster* decision, from 1989 through 1992, the bishops directly attacked prochoice Catholic candidates and officeholders at every level. They excoriated prochoice public servants from the pulpit, barred them from speaking in churches, and threatened excommunication and other sanctions (see page 19). But these tactics backfired. Catholic candidates stood up to the pressure, and they usually won their races. The principles and strategies employed by Catholic politicians in such showdowns reflected an understanding of Catholic tradition and theology itself, as political scientist Mary Segers explains (see page 24).

While the bishops have every right—and perhaps even a responsibility—to engage in public debate, US tax law draws a bright line around political activities that are prohibited for tax-exempt organizations from the parish church to the United States Catholic Conference/

The Catholic vote is becoming the jump ball of American politics. Whoever comes down with that ball usually wins in November.

Ralph Reed, executive director, the Christian Coalition, April 1996

In part because the church's teachings do not fit comfortably with either Democratic or Republican ideology, the Catholic vote has become one of the most contested prizes in politics.

David Broder, *Washington Post*, November 1995

National Conference of Catholic Bishops (see page 31). Such organizations are prohibited by the tax code from "intervening in a political campaign on behalf of or in opposition to candidates for public office." The bishops' vehement opposition to legal abortion, along with the centrality of the issue in electoral campaigns, is in tension with the law, and it has led at times to outright defiance. During the 1980 presidential race, a San Antonio diocesan newspaper, *Today's Catholic*, rated Ronald Reagan "the only presidential candidate who is clearly opposed to abortion." The editorial noted that the IRS had warned that tax-exempt organizations' newspapers could not attempt to influence voters on controversial campaign issues such as abortion—and its headline read, "To the IRS—'nuts'!!!"

In the current campaign, the bishops have seized upon the president's veto of legislation that would have banned one method of late-term abortion. While the bill, if enacted, would not have prevented a single abortion, church leaders embarked on an all-out campaign against Clinton. The effort has included a virtually unprecedented letter to a president from all eight cardinals in the United States, advertisements in major newspapers, and an initiative launched in Catholic churches to generate twenty-seven million postcards to members of Congress, urging them to override the veto. The hierarchy's vow to do everything possible to save the legislation, along with their vigorous castigation of Clinton, pushed talk of the Catholic vote from political back rooms onto the front page.

Journalists across the country leapt to a simple—though incorrect—conclusion, reflected in newspaper headlines: "Clinton Vetoes Catholic Voters," a *Washington Post* column declared. "Clinton's Abortion-Ban Veto Risks Catholic Vote," a *USA Today* headline asserted. It would be hard to argue that such actions by prominent religious leaders have no impact on the political scene. But despite the headlines, it would be even more difficult to make a case that the cardinals will sway Catholics in the voting booth. In a *Los Angeles Times* poll just after the veto, 66 percent of Catholics said the veto would make no difference in their choice between Clinton and Dole—or would make them more likely to vote for Clinton. The inability of church leaders to herd Catholics into a voting bloc has led at least one political commentator to maintain that "there is no 'Catholic vote.'"

There are, however, "millions of Catholics who vote." They are concentrated in the Northeast and Midwest, among the hardest-fought battlegrounds of presidential elections (see page 4). Catholics are active on election day: composing 23 percent of the US population in 1994, Catholics made up 29 percent of voters in US House races that year. And poll after poll shows that most Catholics are prochoice. Only 10 to 15 percent of Catholics agree with the bishops' position that abortion should be illegal in all cases. As voters, Catholics do not follow the bishops—they make up their own minds (see page 6).

There was a time when the leadership of the church could be counted on to reflect—if not deliver—the votes of most Catholics. Until some time in the 1960s, the social gospel of the church, with its heavy emphasis on labor and economic issues, was consistent with the self-interest and values of Catholics, who were then a largely ethnic, working-class group. As the century ends, much has changed. American politics are imbued with cultural and social concerns, and, politically, the church focuses mainly on sexual and reproductive health issues—an area where Catholics and the church leadership have well-documented disagreements. At the same time, the demographics of Catholics, and thus their political interests and inclinations, have changed. Catholics are now more likely than Protestants to be white-collar workers, are just as likely to be college graduates, and have, on average, a higher income.

The rift between the bishops and the Catholic in the pew runs the gamut of public policy matters. While Catholics are clearly more liberal than the bishops on personal morality—being just as likely as other Americans to get divorced, use birth control, and have abortions—most Catholics take a more conservative stance than the bishops on issues such as the death penalty, immigration, and welfare policy.

But the bishops have put abortion far ahead of any other public policy matter, a decision that particularly troubles progressive Catholics this election year, when voters will decide whether the current Congress's deliberate unraveling of the social safety net—a trend the bishops oppose—should or should not continue. The bishops, Byrnes writes, "have to be aware of the ways in which politically weighted actions like the letter to Clinton can indirectly advance a partisan political program that goes well beyond opposition to legal abortion."

This publication presents information and analysis to help readers better understand the place of Catholics—laypeople and leadership—in the 1996 elections. Awareness of the role of religion and religious institutions in the political process is inevitably heightened in this, an election year. Many religious institutions, including the Catholic hierarchy, participate in the political life of the country on an ongoing basis, and insights drawn from religious values can play an important, positive role in the development of public policy. Yet the democratic process is best served when both religious and political leaders understand that their insights will be evaluated on their merits and should compete on equal terms with other positions in the public square. During the campaign season, that competition will best serve the public if religious leaders, politicians, and the press keep in view who Catholic voters are—and what "the Catholic vote" is not. ⊕

Whichever way they [white Catholics] flow, to some extent, determines the election. They are the quintessential swing voters.

Alan Hertzke, political scientist and author of *Representing God in Washington*, November 1995

Everybody knows the Catholic vote is the one most up for grabs on either side.

Don Devine, consultant to the Dole campaign, February 1996

Roman Catholics, State by State

State	Electoral College Votes	Catholics as Percentage of Population	Number of Catholics, in Thousands
Alabama	9	3	137
Alaska	3	9	52
Arizona	8	17	678
Arkansas	6	3	84
California	54	21	7,967
Colorado	8	15	527
Connecticut	8	41	1,354
Delaware	3	17	116
District of Columbia	3	12	75
Florida	25	14	1,953
Georgia	13	4	281
Hawaii	4	20	233
Idaho	4	10	115
Illinois	22	31	3,632
Indiana	12	13	728
Iowa	7	19	520
Kansas	6	16	380
Kentucky	8	10	351
Louisiana	9	31	1,340
Maine	4	20	244
Maryland	10	17	831
Massachusetts	12	50	3,024
Michigan	18	23	2,185
Minnesota	10	26	1,184
Mississippi	7	4	109
Missouri	11	16	841
Montana	3	15	125
Nebraska	5	22	346
Nevada	4	29	433
New Hampshire	4	28	322

Besides California, Clinton will have to focus his efforts on the Northeast and the industrial Midwest if he wants to win. Catholics are very important in those regions.

William Prendergast, author of Catholics and the Republican Party, 1854-1992, February 1996

If I were advising the Clinton White House ... I'd say you guys need to pay attention to the Catholic vote.... You really need that because you're going to have real trouble with white Protestants.

John Green, University of Akron, November 1995

State	Electoral College Votes	Catholics as Percentage of Population	Number of Catholics, in Thousands
New Jersey	15	41	3,243
New Mexico	5	24	422
New York	33	39	7,220
North Carolina	14	3	215
North Dakota	3	26	167
Ohio	21	20	2,217
Oklahoma	8	4	140
Oregon	7	10	308
Pennsylvania	23	30	3,600
Rhode Island	4	64	645
South Carolina	8	3	105
South Dakota	3	22	158
Tennessee	11	3	154
Texas	32	23	4,180
Utah	5	4	78
Vermont	3	25	147
Virginia	13	7	564
Washington	11	10	519
West Virginia	5	6	106
Wisconsin	11	31	1,565
Wyoming	3	10	47

NOTES ON THE DATA

Figures exclude Eastern Rite Catholics and the Military Archdiocese.

Sources of Catholic data: *The Official Catholic Directory, 1996*, New Providence, NJ: P.J. Kenedy & Sons/R.R. Bowker, 1996; and Association of Statisticians of American Religious Bodies, *Churches and Church Membership in the United States, 1990*, Atlanta: Glenmary Research Center, 1992.

The Official Catholic Directory is the source for all states except Delaware, the District of Columbia, and Maryland. The *Directory* reports data by diocese, and a few dioceses cross state lines. Specifically, the dioceses of Wilmington, Delaware, and Washington, DC, include large portions of Maryland, skewing the *Directory*'s data for all three states. Data for those three states therefore were obtained from *Churches and Church Membership*, although these figures are several years older than those in the *Directory*.

In addition, the diocese of Gallup, New Mexico, includes a large area of Arizona. The data for those two states, taken from *The Official Catholic Directory*, therefore might slightly overstate New Mexico's Catholic population and understate Arizona's—but the discrepancy is small enough that the data from the latest *Official Catholic Directory* appear to be at least as reliable as the older data from *Churches and Church Membership*. Finally, two other dioceses—Norwich, Connecticut, and Cheyenne, Wyoming—include minute portions of other states, too small to distort the figures noticeably.

It's not only [Catholics'] numbers but where they're located. They're in the big-ticket states.

Thomas Reese, SJ, senior fellow, Woodstock Theological Seminary, April 1996

The challenge for our church is to be principled without being ideological, to be political without being soft, to be involved without being used. Our moral framework does not easily fit the categories of right or left, Republican or Democrat.

US Catholic bishops' Statement on Political Responsibility for the 1996 election cycle.

The Catholic Vote and Abortion

Poll after poll shows that most Catholics are prochoice. And as voters, they do not follow the bishops—Catholics make up their own minds.

Number of Catholics in the United States: 60 million

Catholics as a portion of total US population: 22%

Catholics as a portion of voters in US House races on Election Day, 1994: 29%

US Catholics who say abortion should be legal in some or all circumstances: 82%

US Catholics who say abortion never can be a morally acceptable choice: 13%

US Catholics saying that a Catholic can vote in good conscience for candidates who support legal abortion: 70%

Importance of abortion in Catholics' voting decisions in the 1994 House races: 9th out of 11 priorities

---

Catholics say abortion should be legal

- A full 82% of US Catholics say abortion should be legal either under certain circumstances or without restrictions.
- This is close to the figure for all Americans: 87%.
- Among Catholics, 39% say a woman should be able to get an abortion if she decides she wants one, no matter what the reason.
- Another 43% say abortion should be legal under certain circumstances, such as when a woman's health is endangered or when a pregnancy results from rape.
- Only 15% of Catholics agree with the bishops' position that abortion should be illegal in all circumstances.

Time/CNN nationwide poll of 1,000 adults, conducted by Yankelovich Partners, Sept. 27-28, 1995, MOE ±3%; subsample of 500 Catholics, MOE ±4.5%.

This finding holds true across polls and over time

- 73% of self-described "progressive" Catholics say abortion should be generally available or available with restrictions.
- 43% of self-described "traditional" Catholics say abortion should be generally available or available with restrictions.
- Only 10% of Catholics (and 10% of all Americans) agree with the bishops' position that abortion should be illegal in all cases.

Pew Research Center for People and the Press, June 1996 Religion Survey, May 31-June 9, 1996, and telephone surveys, July 1994-Oct. 1995, of 4,247 adults, MOE ±3%; subsample of 973 Catholics, MOE ±4%; subsamples of 212 progressive and 237 traditional Catholics, approx. MOE ±10%

- In 1992, 84% of Catholics (and 84% of all Americans) said abortion should be legal in some or all circumstances.
- Only 13% of Catholics agreed with the bishops that abortion should be illegal in all circumstances.

Gallup Survey, for Catholics Speak Out, of 802 Catholics, May 5-7, 1992, MOE ±4%; and Gallup poll of 1,001 adults nationally, Jan. 16-19, 1992, MOE ±3% (data provided by the Roper Center, University of Connecticut).

- In 1990, 85% of Catholics (and 90% of all Americans) said abortion should be legal in at least some circumstances.

- 51% of Catholics, like 57% of all Americans, said choices on abortion should be left up to the woman and her doctor.
- Only 12% of Catholics took the bishops' position that abortion should always be illegal.
  Wall Street Journal/NBC News poll of 1,555 registered voters nationwide, conducted by Peter Hart and Robert Teeter, July 6-10, 1990, MOE ±2.6%; subsample of 427 Catholics, MOE ±5%.

- In 1989, 83% of Catholics (and 83% of all adults) said abortion should be legal, at least in cases of rape/incest or to save the woman's life.
- Among Catholics, only 13% said abortion should always be illegal.
  CBS News/New York Times poll of 1,347 adults, Sept. 17-20, 1989, MOE ±3%; subsample of 341 Catholics, MOE ±5%.

Catholics believe abortion can be moral

- 64% of Catholics, like 68% of all adults, disapprove or strongly disapprove of the statement that abortion is morally wrong in every case.
  US News & World Report survey of 1,000 American adults, conducted by Market Facts' Telenation, designed by Lake Research and Tarrance Group, Sept. 23-24, 1995, MOE ±3.5%; subsample of 493 Catholics, MOE 4.5%.

- Only 13% of Catholics say abortion never can be a morally acceptable choice.
  Gallup Survey, for Catholics Speak Out, of 802 Catholics, May 5-7, 1992, MOE ±4%.

- 69% of Catholics believe a woman who has an abortion for reasons other than to save her life can still be a good Catholic.
  ABC/Washington Post poll of 1,530 adults, conducted by Chilton Research Services, Sept. 28-Oct. 1, 1995, MOE ±3%.

Catholic women have abortions

- Catholic women are as likely as women in the general population to have an abortion.
- Even after standardizing for age and excluding nonwhites and Hispanics (who have higher abortion rates), Catholics are 29 percent more likely than Protestants to have abortions.
  Stanley K. Henshaw & Kathryn Kost (Alan Guttmacher Institute), Family Planning Perspectives, vol. 28, no. 4 (July/Aug. 1996), based on an AGI survey of 9,985 women obtaining abortions in 1994-95.

- The same pattern prevailed in 1987-1988.
- When asked why they were having abortions, Catholics were 8% more likely than those of different religious beliefs to say they did not want others to find out about their sexual activity or pregnancy.
  Stanley K. Henshaw & Jane Silverman (Alan Guttmacher Institute), Family Planning Perspectives, vol. 20, no. 4 (July/Aug. 1988), based on an AGI survey of 9,480 women obtaining abortions in 1987 and an AGI survey of 1,900 women obtaining abortions in 1987-88.

Catholics are not as motivated by abortion as people would think. Some say outlaw it, but there is no consensus.

Tony Fabrizio, pollster for the Dole campaign, February 1996

Before our church leaders attempt to influence public policy on the rights of women and issues of sexuality, they should listen to what the Catholic people have to say.

Frances Kissling, president, Catholics for a Free Choice

On abortion as on birth control: Catholics follow their own consciences

- Only 15% of Catholics say a Catholic should always obey official church teachings on such moral issues as birth control and abortion.
- 79% say it is possible for Catholics to make up their own minds on these issues.
- 80% believe it is possible to disagree with the pope on official positions on morality and still be a good Catholic.
  Time/CNN nationwide poll of 1,000 adults, conducted by Yankelovich Partners, Sept. 27-28, 1995, MOE ±3%; subsample of 500 Catholics, MOE ±4.5%.

- In one recent poll, 82% of Catholics disapproved or strongly disapproved of the statement that using artificial birth control, such as condoms or birth control pills, is morally wrong.
- In another poll, 76% of Catholics disagreed with the statement that using artificial means of birth control is wrong.
  82%: US News & World Report survey of 1,000 American adults, conducted by Market Facts' Telenation, designed by Lake Research and Tarrance Group, Sept. 23-24, 1995, MOE ±3.5%; subsample of 493 Catholics, MOE ±4.5%.
  76%: Time/CNN nationwide poll of 1,000 adults, conducted by Yankelovich Partners, Sept. 27-28, 1995, MOE ±3%; subsample of 500 Catholics, MOE ±4.5%.

Catholics go to the polls

- Number of Catholics in the United States: 60 million
- Catholics as a portion of the total US population: 22%
  PJ Kenedy & Sons, Official Catholic Directory 1996 (New Providence, NJ: R.R. Bowker, 1996).

- Catholics as a portion of voters who turned out in 1992 on Election Day: 27%
- Catholics, among all voters turning out to vote for US House candidates on Election Day in 1994: 29%
  Voter News Service (formerly Voter Research & Surveys) exit polls, 1992 & 1994.

- 77% of US Catholics are registered to vote—just under the 79% registered in the general population.
- 50% of Catholics are among the voters judged "most likely" to vote in the November 1996 elections (on the basis of answers to several questions about voting habits and plans).
- Those "most likely" to vote include 52% of self-described "traditional" Catholics and 47% of self-described "progressive" Catholics.
- This compares to 49% of the general population, 54% of white evangelical Protestants, and 56% of white mainline Protestants.
  Pew Research Center for People and the Press, June 1996 Religion Survey, May 31-June 9, 1996, and telephone surveys, July 1994-Oct. 1995, of 4,247 adults, MOE ±3%; subsample of 973 Catholics, MOE ±4%; subsamples of 212 progressive and 237 traditional Catholics, approx. MOE ±10%; voter categories were "most likely," "somewhat likely," or "not likely" to vote.

In spite of what you may hear on television and read in national newspapers, there is no "Catholic vote."

Stuart Rothenberg, Roll Call, April 1996

Of course, the Catholic church doesn't control the votes of its members, many of whom support abortion rights, and the Catholic vote is neither monolithic nor determined by a single issue.

Susan Page, USA Today, April 1996

- Every winning presidential candidate since 1976 has carried a majority or plurality of Catholic voters: 54% for Carter in 1976; a 50% plurality for Reagan in 1980; 54% for Reagan in 1984; 52% for Bush in 1988; and a 44% plurality for Clinton in 1992.
Exit Polls: 1976, CBS; 1980-1988, CBS/New York Times; 1992, Voter News Service.

- In the 1994 House and Senate races, 52% of Catholic voters favored Republicans. In House races alone, 51% voted for Democrats.
- In all House and Senate races, 60% of Protestant voters and 60% of self-identified "religious right" voters favored Republicans.
- Wealthier Catholics were likelier than other Catholics to vote for Republican House and Senate candidates.
- Most Catholics with postgraduate education, or less than a college degree, did not vote Republican. Most of those with a college degree, and no more, did vote Republican.
Roper Center for Public Opinion Research, America at the Polls: 1994.

Abortion is not a litmus test—but Catholics vote prochoice

- Only 9% of US Catholics feel so strongly about abortion that they would not vote for a political candidate who disagreed with their opinion, regardless of the candidate's stand on other issues.
- This compares to 12% of all Americans.
CBS News/New York Times poll of 1,200 adults, May 31-June 3, 1996, MOE ±3%; subsample of 294 Catholics, MOE ±6%.

- Rank of abortion among 11 priorities Catholics considered in deciding how to vote in the 1994 US House races: 9.
- Rank of abortion for all voters: tied for 8-9
- 39% of Catholics said crime was among their top two priorities, while only 13% cited abortion among the top two.
- Catholics ranked the 11 issues in this order: crime, the economy/jobs, health care, taxes, national issues tied with education, family values/morality, local issues, abortion, campaign finance reform, foreign trade/NAFTA.
Mitofsky International, Nov. 8, 1994, total sample 5,260, including more than 1,000 Catholics.

- The pattern was similar in the 1992 presidential race, with 46% of Catholics saying the economy was among the two most important issues, and only 9% naming abortion.
Voter News Service (then Voter Research & Surveys), exit polls, 1992.

- 66% of Catholics say President Clinton's April 1996 veto of the bill to ban a late-term abortion method will make no difference in their choice between Clinton and Bob Dole in the presidential election—or will make them more likely to vote for Clinton.
- Just after Clinton vetoed the late-term abortion bill, Catholics preferred Clinton over Dole by 58% to 33%.
Los Angeles Times poll of 1,374 adults (1,149 registered voters), Apr. 13-16, 1996, MOE ±3%; Catholic subsample 418, MOE ±5%.

Though Catholic clergy speak out frequently against abortion from the pulpit, Catholic voters do not use abortion as their litmus test. They give President Clinton, who favors abortion rights, high approval ratings and are the most inclined of all groups to vote for Clinton over... Dole in 1996 (62 percent vs. 33 percent).

Laurie Goodstein, *Washington Post*, June 1996

- Just after the late-term abortion bill veto, Catholic women, who make up 26% of the female electorate, favored Clinton over Dole by a 61% to 35% margin.
  Greenberg/Lake survey of 1089 registered voters, for Emily's List, Apr. 12, 1996.

- 70% of Catholics agree or strongly agree with the statement that Catholics can, in good conscience, vote for political candidates who support legal abortion.
  Gallup Survey, for Catholics Speak Out, of 802 Catholics, May 5-7, 1992, MOE ±4%.

Catholics say religion should not dictate politics

> *[Church leaders] can no more deliver the Catholic vote than the labor unions can deliver the labor vote. We're dealing with an adult citizenry that makes up its own mind while looking at a large number of issues.*
>
> Thomas Reese, SJ, senior fellow, Woodstock Theological Seminary, April 1996

- 77% of Catholics, like 72% of all Americans, say it is not appropriate for religious leaders to urge people to vote for a candidate because of his or her stand on abortion.
- 63% of all Republicans and 73% of all Democrats say it is not appropriate.
  CBS News/New York Times poll of 1,200 adults, May 31-June 3, 1996, MOE ±3%.

- 56% of Catholics (and 55% of non-Catholics) say it is appropriate for religious leaders to take a public position on abortion.
- But 68% of Catholics say it is not appropriate for religious leaders to urge people to vote for or against a candidate because of his or her stand on abortion.
- 65% of non-Catholics say it is not appropriate.
  New York Times/CBS News poll of 1,536 adults nationwide, Sept. 18-22, 1995, MOE ±3%; subsample of 423 Catholics, MOE ±5%.

- Just before the 1995 papal visit, 73% of US Catholics said that knowing the pope's position on a social or political issue would not influence their position on the issue.
- Only 16% said they would be more likely to support the pope's position.
  New York Times/CBS News poll of 1,536 adults nationwide, Sept. 18-22, 1995, MOE ±3%; subsample of 423 Catholics, MOE ±5%.

- 79% of Catholics say they are not members or followers of conservative Christian political groups.
  Peter D. Hart Research Associates, national survey, for People For the American Way, of 1,252 registered voters, July 19-22, 1995; subsample of 279 Catholics, MOE ±6.3%.

The Bishops, Abortion, and Presidential Politics

By Timothy A. Byrnes

The political meaning of the American Catholic hierarchy's activities is determined both by the nature of those activities themselves, and by the specific political context in which those activities take place. The bishops determine their own agenda and priorities. But they do not determine on their own the ways in which that agenda and those priorities will intersect with the rhetoric of American national politics or with the competition between particular political candidates at any given time.

In this article, I will examine these dynamic intersections between the bishops' agenda and American politics and make two closely related arguments. First, I will argue that the bishops' political agenda, determined by the form that their particular statements take, and by the emphasis those statements imply, has been headed for over two decades by the single issue of abortion. Second, I will contend that this abortion-centered agenda, given the specific political context in which the bishops have pursued it over the last twenty-five years, has established for the Catholic hierarchy a prominent and, regrettably, partisan role in the American political arena. These arguments will allow us to consider the hierarchy's most recent political intervention from the appropriate historical perspective.

In April of this year, President Clinton vetoed a bill that would have outlawed a method of late-term pregnancy termination called "intact dilation and extraction" by the medical community and its supporters and "partial-birth abortion" by its opponents. The president vetoed the bill because it did not include an exception to the ban for cases in which the women's health would be harmed by carrying the pregnancy to term. On April 16, the eight Roman Catholic cardinals in the United States, along with the president of the National Conference of Catholic Bishops, wrote a letter to the president strenuously protesting his veto. Terming Clinton's decision "shameful" and "beyond comprehension," they pledged to do all they could in the coming months to inform people of the issue and to encourage "Catholics and other people of good will" to urge Congress to override the president's veto.

In one sense, this action by the leaders of the American Catholic church was virtually unprecedented; very rarely had such a letter ever been sent by all of the American cardinals to an American president. However, the letter's near-uniqueness in this one regard should not blind us to how consistent this letter is with the American hierarchy's political activities over the last two decades. It is a break with tradition in terms of procedure. But in terms of content, the political priorities

---

Timothy A. Byrnes is an associate professor of political science at Colgate University. He is the author of Catholic Bishops in American Politics *(1991) and coeditor of* The Catholic Church and the Politics of Abortion *(1992) and* Abortion Politics in American States *(1995). This article originally appeared in* Conscience, *Summer 1996.*

it implies, and the ways in which it intersects with the rhetoric and agenda of national electoral politics, the letter is familiar stuff indeed.

A is for Abortion

Since the Second Vatican Council charged the bishops with reading the "signs of the times" and applying the lessons of the Gospels to contemporary American society, the American Catholic bishops have been active participants in our national political debate. Most particularly, they have applied traditional Catholic moral teaching to the range of what have come to be called the life issues. The bishops have opposed abortion, to be sure, but they have also opposed capital punishment, euthanasia, the use of nuclear weapons, and threats to the dignity and sustenance of the poor. Cardinal Joseph Bernardin, in particular, has spoken often of complex relationships between and among these various issues, and of the need for the church to retain a commitment to what he has called the consistent ethic or "seamless garment" of respect for human life.

Along another, more explicitly political track, however, the church's leaders have not been quite so consistent. Owing to both the style of their statements and activities on abortion, and to the clear distinction between that style and their approach to all other issues, the bishops have communicated over and over again that abortion is their leading political priority.

Every four years, the NCCB releases a document, called the political responsibility statement, in which the bishops (a) encourage American Catholics to participate in the upcoming presidential election and (b) offer a long list of official conference policy positions based on the bishops' application of Catholic teaching to the issues of the day. Since this list is always offered in alphabetical order, abortion, not surprisingly, has appeared at the top. But it is more than an accident of alphabetization that has established abortion as the Catholic hierarchy's first political priority; it is also the varied and imaginative ways in which the bishops have emphasized abortion over all other issues just when political circumstances have drawn the most public attention to the hierarchy and its agenda.

The hierarchy's collective denunciations of abortion are more strident and more straightforwardly political than their statements concerning any other issue. And perhaps more importantly, the connections that various bishops draw between the issue of abortion on the one hand and electoral politics on the other are consistently more direct and more pointed than the connections drawn in terms of any other issue on the hierarchy's agenda.

The 1976 presidential election between Gerald Ford and Jimmy Carter was the first national campaign to follow the Supreme Court's decision in *Roe v. Wade*. It was therefore a seminal event in establishing the role that abortion would play on the American Catholic hierarchy's political agenda. The NCCB's political responsibility statement of that year argued that "the church's concern for human rights and social justice should be comprehensive and consistent," covering "a broad range of topics on which the bishops of the US have already expressed themselves." But when the time came for the conference's spokesmen to comment publicly on the church's agenda and its relationship to the election campaign, their approach was anything but comprehensive and consistent. Joseph Bernardin, then the archbishop of Cincinnati and the NCCB's

> It is more than an accident of alphabetization that has established abortion as the hierarchy's first political priority, ahead of Head Start and Medicaid.

president, focused his public comments squarely on the single issue of abortion.

Most pointedly, and now most famously, Bernardin announced after meetings between the presidential candidates and the NCCB's executive committee that he and the other bishops were "disappointed" in Carter's position on abortion, but "encouraged" by Ford's. These statements conveyed the great importance that the bishops placed on the issue of abortion. But it was Bernardin's silence on the political ramifications of all of the other issues in the campaign that cemented the impression that abortion mattered most to the Catholic hierarchy. Apparently the bishops were neither "disappointed" in Ford's disagreements with them on matters other than abortion, nor "encouraged" by their areas of agreement with Carter.

Bernardin himself offered the rationale for the bishops' overriding emphasis on abortion in 1976. "If the church seems particularly concerned about abortion at the moment," he said, "it is for this reason: if we become insensitive to the violation of the basic human right to life, our sensitivity to the entire spectrum of human rights will ultimately be eroded."

Since these events of 1976, the elected leadership of the bishops' conference has tried not to get so directly involved in electoral politics. Indeed, in response to the controversy surrounding his participation in the 1976 campaign, Bernardin himself has sought both to place abortion within a broader context of consistent respect for human life, and to soften the sharp political edge of the church's steadfast opposition to abortion. The problem, however, is that while Bernardin has given speeches and sermons on the seamless garment, and while the conference staff has stoutly refrained from commenting on individual candidates, some of the most prominent members of the National Conference of Catholic Bishops have done everything in their power to establish abortion as, in the words of Cardinal Law of Boston, "the critical issue of the moment."

Over the last twenty years, these individual bishops have banned prochoice speakers from Catholic institutions and functions, threatened the excommunication of prochoice public officials, singled out prochoice politicians for election-year criticism, and explicitly advised Catholic voters to eschew prochoice candidates. At the same time, of course, these same bishops have turned a deaf ear to the issues on which prolife candidates and officials might disagree with the NCCB's other public policy positions.

The bishops' much publicized pastoral letters on nuclear weapons ("The Challenge of Peace") and the American economy ("Economic Justice for All"), for example, both frontally challenged central policies and practices of the Reagan-Bush administration. In fact, the release of the two letters did cause substantial friction and debate between the bishops' conference and the Republican administration. But in the context of electoral politics, wherein no national candidates share the bishops' whole agenda, the pastoral letters were clearly overshadowed by the bishops' opposition to abortion.

In the 1984 campaign, for example, Ronald Reagan was received repeatedly by Catholic bishops for meetings and genial photo opportunities. In not a single instance that I am aware of did any of these bishops take the opportunity to challenge Reagan to defend defense policies or economic policies that flew directly in the face of the NCCB's positions. During the same campaign, on the other hand, Walter Mondale pointedly avoided any meetings with Catholic bishops because he knew perfectly well that such

> The Catholic bishops' consistent and consistently creative emphasis on abortion was a godsend for the Republican party.

meetings would focus on his disagreement with the hierarchy over abortion. Indeed, while Reagan was smiling and dining with bishop after bishop, Mondale's Catholic running mate, Geraldine Ferraro, was engaged in a pitched debate with the archbishop of New York concerning the church's "monolithic" opposition to abortion.

The salient point here is not merely that some members of the hierarchy have placed a particularly pointed emphasis on the church's opposition to abortion. It is rather that the willingness of these vocal bishops to relate the church's position on abortion directly to partisan politics, combined with the complete absence of such willingness on the part of any other bishops in regard to any other issue, creates over time an impression that abortion really is more central than any other issue or any purportedly consistent ethic.

Consider again the hierarchy's response to President Clinton's veto in April, and place that response in the context of recent political developments in Washington and across the country. Newt Gingrich and the Republican majority in the House have launched frontal assaults on welfare guarantees and government entitlements that have long enjoyed the support of the Catholic hierarchy. Bob Dole has pushed a multi-billion-dollar reinvigoration of a Strategic Defense Initiative that the bishops have criticized as wasteful and destabilizing. And politicians of every partisan stripe have tripped over themselves to find ever more criminal offenses deserving of a death penalty that the bishops have opposed for years. To be sure, all of these issues have been the subject of public statements and lobbying on the part of bishops and their staff. But only one issue was deemed worthy of the unprecedented act of a collective letter signed by the most prominent and highly ranking members of the national conference. The most public and powerful political tools at the hierarchy's disposal were carefully reserved, as they have always been, for abortion.

This emphasis on abortion is particularly significant in 1996. Just as 1976 was the first presidential election to follow *Roe v. Wade*, so 1996 is the first presidential campaign to follow the "Republican Revolution" of 1994. Bob Dole and Republican candidates across the country will run this year on a platform and a legislative record that are sharply opposed to much of the spirit and letter of the bishops' political responsibility statements. Threats to programs like Head Start and Medicaid, for example, are more serious now than at any time since those program began decades ago. Given the anti-social-welfare program being advanced by the Republican party this year, the Catholic bishops have to consider particularly carefully the place they give to abortion on their own public agenda. They have to be aware of the ways in which politically weighted actions like the letter to Clinton can indirectly advance a partisan political program that goes well beyond opposition to legal abortion.

Indeed, in some ways the cardinals' letter to President Clinton harkens back to 1976 when it was the formal leadership of the bishops' conference, rather than individual bishops, who stressed the primacy of abortion. The collective letter to Clinton, explicitly political in tone, once again formally places the issue of abortion in the center, as deserving of the church's special and particularly pointed emphasis. I am not arguing that the bishops should not oppose Clinton's veto of the abortion bill. That is their right, and given the church hierarchy's position on abortion, perhaps even their responsibility. What I am arguing, however, is that the bishops' response

> Keeping Pat Buchanan and the Republican Coalition for Choice seated quietly together at a national political convention is a job only for the most nimble of contortionists.

to the veto, in this particular way, in this particular political context, conveys the message, just as Bernardin did in 1976, that the church is "particularly concerned about abortion at the moment."

The Power of Political Context

As I noted at the beginning, the political significance of the bishops' agenda is set not only by the bishops' presentation of it, but also by the political context in which it is advanced. If the bishops decided to emphasize their opposition to birth control as a political issue, for example, it is unlikely that such an effort would have much direct political significance. To be sure, the bishops could use the impressive institutional resources at their disposal to raise the profile of birth control as an issue of debate in American society. But the lack of any large constituency in support of the church's position on birth control and the slim chance that any major political party or candidate would come along to do the church's bidding on the issue mean that opposition to birth control would probably not come to dominate the church's participation in politics, regardless of the emphasis the bishops might give to it.

The case is entirely different with abortion, however. For one thing, there is a large, well organized constituency, both inside and outside the church, deeply committed to opposing legal abortion. Moreover, one of the major political parties, the Republican party, has not only adopted opposition to abortion into its platform, but also placed abortion at the center of a major political strategy designed to bring about long-term change in the alignment of American politics.

From 1932 until 1968 or 1972, American politics was dominated by the Democratic party's New Deal coalition. Made up most prominently of Catholics, Jews, Northern blacks, Southern whites, and labor union members, this coalition was brought together by the support all its various factions offered to Franklin Roosevelt and the New Deal. There were deep divisions within the coalition, most obviously between Southern whites and Northern blacks (Southern blacks for all practical purposes couldn't vote), but its shared economic interests, broadly speaking, and the political skill of FDR and his successors were able to hold the party together for several decades.

By the late 1960s, however, the New Deal coalition was showing its age as the internal divisions within the Democratic party began to rival in political salience the partisan divisions between Democrats and Republicans. All of the storied political dramas of the 1960s, after all, took place pretty much within the Democratic party. The Civil Rights struggle, in particular, was a battle between Democratic blacks and recalcitrant Democratic white political elites in Southern state capitals and Washington, DC. Similarly, the fight over the Vietnam War was mostly confined to the Democratic party. It is easy to forget now that most of the hawks in hardhats were Democrats, at least before 1972.

The explosive end of the New Deal coalition as a national electoral force came in 1968. The dramatic social and cultural rifts within the party were played out on television at the Democratic convention in Chicago. And the deep racial divisions led that year to the defection of George Wallace and the old Solid South from the Democratic fold. Richard Nixon was elected president in 1968 because the Democrats imploded, and he and Republican political strategists set out following his election to strengthen and further their advantage. The problem for

> Threats to programs like Head Start and Medicaid are more serious now than at any time since those programs began decades ago.

> With social welfare programs under threat, the Catholic bishops have to consider carefully the place they give to abortion on their own public agenda.

Nixon, and indeed for all his Republican successors, is that they had to work to further weaken the Democratic base without directly addressing the issue that was for decades a major fault line in the Democratic party—race. Nixon and his successors could surely reap the benefits of the racial division of the Democratic coalition, and they could even nudge those divisions along whenever possible. But as the standard bearers of the "Party of Lincoln," and not segregationists themselves, they could not, as George Wallace could, run a straightforwardly racial campaign.

For that reason, and also because politics is the art of exploiting division, Republican candidates went in search of other "wedge issues" that could further divide the Democratic party against itself. In that pursuit, the Republicans turned in the 1970s and 1980s to issues like crime, patriotism, and of course, abortion. Abortion was, from the 1972 through 1988 presidential campaigns, an issue that "worked" for the Republican party and its candidates. Each Republican presidential candidate since Richard Nixon has used abortion to assert both his own commitment to family and religious values, and his opponent's purported abandonment of religious principle and moral grounding. I have no doubt, by the way, that many of these candidates sincerely opposed the practice of elective abortion in the United States. But I also have no doubt that abortion was throughout this period at the heart of the Republican party's concerted effort to exacerbate the already deep cultural divisions tearing at the Democratic party.

In this very specific context, in which social and religious issues had a particularly high political profile, the Catholic bishops' consistent and consistently creative emphasis on abortion was a godsend for the Republican party. The reason that Bernardin's "disappointment" in Jimmy Carter was so politically significant in 1976 was that Carter, at that very moment, was trying to prevent a rift from opening between himself and the Catholic voters he needed to patch the tattered New Deal coalition back together. The reason that Cardinal O'Connor's public feud with Geraldine Ferraro over abortion so troubled the Democratic ticket in 1984 was that Walter Mondale, at that moment, was arguing that Ronald Reagan and the Republican party did not have a monopoly on virtue, or exclusive access to God's ear.

The emphasis that the Catholic hierarchy has given to abortion, particularly when politicians, the press, and voters have been paying the most attention, has intersected with the rhetoric of national politics and with conservative political strategies to suggest a close fit between the teachings of the American Catholic hierarchy and the policies of the modern Republican party. But that suggestion is not supported by any careful analysis of the actual relationship between the NCCB's political responsibility statements and the Republican party's electoral platforms.

A New Era in Abortion Politics

In 1989, the political context surrounding the issue of abortion was transformed rather dramatically by the Supreme Court's decision in *Webster v. Reproductive Health Services, Inc.* In that decision, the court upheld a number of restrictive provisions of a Missouri antiabortion law and sent a clear signal to state legislatures that the court was willing to countenance restrictions that did not conform to the trimester framework originally laid down in *Roe*. The main political effects of *Webster* were, one, an explosion of state legislative activity meant to test the limits of the court's new opening and, two, the reinvigoration of a prochoice movement anxious to defend its gains against new attacks.

Prochoice forces within the Republican party were particularly energized by the court's decision in *Webster*. It was one thing, apparently, for prochoice Republicans to accept the recruitment of prolife conservatives into their party, and even for them to acquiesce in a prolife Republican platform, when the right to abortion was securely protected by *Roe* and the Supreme Court. But once the court began to chip away at the fundamental right to an abortion established by *Roe*, and once prolife forces within the Republican party began to call in response for more state-level antiabortion legislation, prochoice Republicans began to speak up, loudly.

The legalization of elective abortion had originally driven a wedge into the Democratic party, but after 1989 and *Webster*, the prospect of recriminalizing abortion began to dig into the coalition that the Republicans had worked so hard to build under Nixon and Reagan. The chasm that abortion revealed between social and economic conservatives in the GOP does not rival in intensity or historic significance the split between civil rights activists and segregationists in the old Democratic party. But it is nevertheless a deeply troubling development for Republican candidates trying to hold their party together. As George Bush would surely attest, keeping Pat Buchanan and the Republican Coalition for Choice seated quietly together at a national political convention is a job only for the most nimble of contortionists.

As the issue of abortion divides the various factions in the Republican party, Republican candidates, particularly candidates for national office, are likely to respond by directing less and less attention to it. The key to political success, after all, is to highlight the divisions among your opponents' supporters and downplay those issues that divide your own. This is exactly what is behind Republican talk of a "big tent" on abortion, and exactly what is driving the efforts of prochoice Republican leaders to eliminate the very mention of the issue from the party's platform altogether. Who would have predicted just ten years ago that one of the Republican presidential nominee's central tasks in the summer of 1996 would be to *prevent* opposition to legal abortion from becoming a major element of his electoral platform?

All of these developments relating to the politics of abortion, of course, have the potential to profoundly influence the role of the Catholic hierarchy in American politics. Just as the deep partisan divisions over abortion in the 1970s and 1980s raised the bishops' political profile and influence, so the quieting of partisan warfare over abortion might lessen substantially the political significance of the bishops' opposition to abortion. The bishops' position on abortion is unlikely to take center political stage in a political era in which the partisan divisions on abortion are narrowing. In time, such an altered political context could even result in greater attention to the NCCB's positions on politically divisive issues other than abortion.

For the time being, however, the controversy over the intact dilation and extraction/partial-birth abortion procedure has added another important wrinkle to the contemporary politics of abortion and trained the political spotlight once again on the Catholic hierarchy. Dole, at the moment before the Republican convention, is trying to ameliorate

> The quieting of partisan warfare over abortion could, in time, result in greater attention to the NCCB's positions on other divisive issues.

disputes within his party over the right to abortion. For now, he would be happy if abortion just went away for a little while as a political issue. But once the conventions are over, once Dole is facing Bill Clinton rather than Pat Buchanan, he and Republican strategists are sure to dust off the issue of abortion, define it publicly in terms of the "partial-birth" controversy, and once again use it to attempt to place their Democratic opponent outside the mainstream of American values and morality. Clinton's veto will allow Dole to disparage the president's values and morality without having to disparage the legal right to an abortion per se.

Moreover, one of the central tools Dole is sure to use in making this argument in the coming months is the letter in which the eight Catholic cardinals, the most prominent leaders of the American Catholic church, called the president's action "shameful" and "beyond comprehension." In fact, the use of the bishops to further this political strategy has already been well established. Dole's speech excoriating Clinton's veto for "pushing the limits of decency too far," for example, was delivered to the annual convention of the Catholic Press Association, and it referred both to the cardinals' letter and to Pope John Paul II's statement opposing the president's veto. And so as to be sure his point would not be missed, Dole followed up the speech with a twenty-minute meeting with Cardinal Anthony Bevilacqua of Philadelphia.

All of this poses a challenge this election year to the American bishops, both collectively and individually. Given the specific political context surrounding abortion at this particular moment, how will the bishops present their public policy agenda? How will they respond to a renewed attempt to draw partisan political advantage from their opposition to abortion? Will they try to counteract a set of circumstances that is likely to limit the scope of their political role in 1996 to the issue of a rarely performed late-term abortion procedure?

All these questions will be answered by the bishops this summer and fall, but for now I will venture a couple of predictions. First of all, the bishops' opposition to intact dilation and extraction/partial-birth abortion, and specifically the letter to President Clinton emphasizing that opposition, will be cited by Bob Dole and other Republicans repeatedly during the election campaign. Indeed, the extent of public discussion of that letter will probably exceed, by several orders of magnitude, the public discussion of the NCCB's position on all other issues combined. In addition, the eight American cardinals and the president of the National Conference of Catholic Bishops will probably refrain from sending any letters to Bob Dole, or even any more letters to Bill Clinton, expressing either outrage or pleasure at the policy positions taken by either candidate on issues unrelated to abortion. My guess is that in terms of setting their priorities in the context of this election year, the cardinals have already had their say. ⊕

> How will the bishops respond to renewed attempts to draw partisan political advantage from their opposition to abortion?

Episodes in Abortion Politics

How the Catholic hierarchy has handled prochoice politicians before

The Catholic bishops' surge into abortion politics in 1996 was as predictable as the timing of the late-term abortion controversy was political. When abortion is a electoral campaign issue, it dictates where the bishops throw their weight in the partisan contest.

Between a high-profile letter from the US cardinals to President Bill Clinton, statements from the National Conference of Catholic Bishops, and a campaign to send twenty-seven million postcards to members of Congress, the bishops have directed all their political clout this year against prochoice public officials, especially the president. Their campaign this year is best understood in the context of election years past.

Since the 1973 *Roe v. Wade* ruling legalized abortion throughout the United States, the institutional Catholic church has played a significant, sometimes principal, role in antiabortion politics. In 1975, the bishops' pastoral plan sought to establish antiabortion activities offices not only in each parish and diocese, but also in each congressional district. The task of these district committees, the plan stated, would be to "organize people to persuade their elected representatives to support a constitutional amendment and other prolife legislation." At times, this aggressive lobbying program spilled over into the electoral process. This was most apparent at the presidential level in 1976, when the bishops met with Jimmy Carter and Gerald Ford, and crowned Ford the acceptable one.

In 1980 a coalition of clergy and prochoice groups, disturbed by such incursions, filed suit to force the Internal Revenue Service to revoke the tax-exempt status of the US Catholic Conference and all other Catholic church organizations. During the ten years in which the case was in the courts, the bishops exercised substantial caution in the electoral arena. This period of comparative calm was interrupted during the 1984 presidential campaign when some prelates, Cardinal John O'Connor of New York in particular, vigorously assailed the prochoice position of Catholic vice presidential candidate Geraldine Ferraro and implicitly urged Catholics to vote for antiabortion candidates.

By 1989 it became apparent that the lawsuit would be dismissed, the Supreme Court opened the door to state laws restricting abortion services, and some of the more conservative bishops began to take a stronger approach to the issue. Archbishop Roger Mahony of Los Angeles issued a statement declaring that Catholic officeholders have an obligation to work to make abortion illegal. Bishop James McHugh of Camden, New Jersey, urged Catholics in a pastoral letter not to tolerate prochoice Catholic public officials. Then, at their annual autumn meeting, the US bishops adopted a "Resolution on Abortion" that reemphasized their determination to prohibit legal abortions and exhorted all Catholics to work to change federal and state abortion laws. The resolution did not spell out a specific strategy, but after its release bishops across the country began pressuring prochoice Catholics, especially those holding public office, to lower their profiles or change their positions.

Americans of all religious persuasions, including Catholic Americans, wrestle with this issue [of late-term abortion]. Many of them are profoundly affected by the moral ambivalence other Americans share. And the President doesn't believe, and I don't know that any of us here at the White House believe, that any particular religious group in America votes monolithically or as a bloc. I think there's ample evidence to, in fact, suggest that they don't.

White House spokesman Mike McCurry, on President Clinton's veto of a bill that would have banned a type of late-term abortion, April 1996

The following chronology is a sampling of the actions by bishops and other representatives of the institutional church against prochoice Catholic public officials—those who were willing to make their cases public. The events here illustrate that the bishops' decision to view the 1996 presidential election above all through the lens of abortion is a political approach with substantial precedents.

November 7, 1989
Providence, Rhode Island
Bishop Louis Gelineau of Providence, Rhode Island, criticizes Rhode Island's Representative Claudine Schneider for her prochoice voting record, declaring that it is "not what the church would expect of a Catholic legislator."

November 15, 1989
San Diego, California
Three weeks before a special run-off election for the California state senate, Bishop Leo Maher prohibits prochoice Catholic candidate Lucy Killea from receiving communion in the Catholic church because of her prochoice position on abortion.

On December 5, Killea beats favored Republican opponent Carol Bentley—tipping the balance in the state senate to a one-vote prochoice majority. Bentley attributes her stunning defeat to Maher's intervention in the political process. She claims the bishop's action made Killea an "international celebrity and a martyr."

November 19-29, 1989
Helena, Montana
Bishops Elden Curtiss of Helena and Anthony Milone of the Great Falls-Billings diocese issue a press release affirming the institutional church's opposition to abortion and exhorting "all Catholics who hold public office in this state to refrain from public statements which contradict ... basic principles of Catholic morality."

Curtiss then meets behind closed doors with prochoice Catholic state auditor Andrea Bennett and asks her not to speak publicly in support of abortion. Curtiss also publicly confronts Nancy Keenan, Montana's superintendent of public education and a prochoice Catholic, about her endorsement of a woman's right to choose abortion. Curtiss asks her to respond in writing to a number of questions.

After being criticized for interrogating Montana's female prochoice Catholic officials, Curtiss summons two male prochoice Catholic officials—Secretary of State Mike Cooney and Supreme Court Clerk Ed Smith—to discuss their public positions on abortion.

November 29, 1989
Providence, Rhode Island
The *Providence Journal* reports that the local diocesan newspaper, the *Providence Visitor*, has imposed an advertising ban under which the *Visitor* will refuse Christmas greetings from politicians who do not sign a statement supporting a constitutional amendment to outlaw abortion.

January 10, 1990
Pennsylvania
A pastor dismisses Republican legislative candidate Rosemary McAvoy from two positions—school board president and lector at Mass—because of her prochoice views. McAvoy goes public with the news in mid-March in order to dispel rumors that she is withdrawing from running for office.

January 17, 1990
Albany, New York
Cardinal John O'Connor of New York and eighteen other Catholic bishops converge on the state capitol to lobby on a variety of issues, including abortion. O'Connor promises that the state's bishops will "agitate constantly" for legislative restrictions on abortion and says it is vital to require Catholic lawmakers to vote their "Catholic" consciences on the issue.

January 23, 1990
New York
Auxiliary Bishop Austin Vaughan, interviewed in jail after an antiabortion protest, proclaims that New York Governor Mario Cuomo is in "serious risk of going to hell" for his prochoice views. He calls Cuomo a "Sunday Catholic" and compares him to a "Nazi soldier" who "may have objected to the Holocaust but nevertheless supported the German government's right to murder six million innocent Jews."

A week later, Cardinal O'Connor defends Vaughan's condemnation of Cuomo, saying the bishop is under "the obligation to warn any Catholic that his soul is at risk if he should die while deliberately pursuing any gravely evil course of action"—such as advocating the view that abortion should be legal.

January 24, 1990
New Orleans
The Archdiocese of New Orleans releases a statement that condemns the taking of prochoice positions on abortion. It is a response to the prochoice positions advocated by Mayor Sidney Barthelemy, a former seminarian, and challenger Donald Mintz at a forum during the city's mayoral race.

February 9, 1990
Indiana
UPI reports that while celebrating Sunday Mass at St. Ann Catholic Church in Kewanna, a parish priest has chastised state representative Robert Sabatini by referring indirectly to Sabatini's prochoice votes in the Indiana House. In response, Sabatini decides to forgo communion at the church. Later, William Higi, bishop of the Lafayette diocese, phones Sabatini to apologize.

February 15, 1990
Pennsylvania
After prochoice Catholic Cliessa Nagle announces that she will be a Democratic candidate for the state house of representatives, parish priest Joseph Murray writes a letter asking her to resign her position as volunteer coordinator of a parish program because of her views on abortion. Writes Murray, "To have someone on our staff publicly advocating a position in direct opposition to the teaching of the Catholic church on a matter so basic and vital would be a source of confusion for our people."

February 20, 1990
New York
Bishop Thomas Daily of Palm Beach, Florida, soon to become bishop of the Diocese of Brooklyn, announces at a news conference that he will ban Brooklyn native Mario Cuomo from speaking in the diocese's churches. At a news conference the next day, Daily modifies his position, indicating that Cuomo will be able to talk in a limited capacity.

The most important issue for Catholics [in 1992] was jobs and the economy; the most important characteristic they wanted in a presidential candidate was the ability to bring about needed change. Catholics were less likely than Protestants to say that abortion or "family values" was one of the one or two issues that mattered most in deciding how they voted.

Jim Castelli, *National Catholic Reporter*, December 1992

Our intention is not either to advance or to undermine the electoral fortunes of any individual or party. When religious leaders enter into electoral politics, it is more likely that religion will be debased than that politics will be elevated.... [Nevertheless] while we do not seek to coerce, neither do we intend to be coerced into silence by those unwilling to recognize the importance of religion and moral truth to the achievement of the common good.

Bishop Anthony Pilla of Cleveland, president of the National Conference of Catholic Bishops, June 1996

March 14, 1990
New York
Cardinal O'Connor, who heads the Committee for Pro-Life Activities of the National Conference of Catholic Bishops (NCCB), writes a letter to every member of Congress pledging to launch a massive lobbying effort against legislation protecting a woman's right to choose abortion. The letter, attacking the Freedom of Choice Act and the Reproductive Health Equity Act, is accompanied by a picture of a fetus, purportedly at eighteen weeks gestation.

March 19, 1990
Guam
Governor Joseph Ada of Guam signs into law the most restrictive abortion legislation in any US state or territory, prohibiting abortion except when the life of the mother is threatened. During legislative debate on the proposal, Archbishop Anthony Apuron had threatened to excommunicate any Catholic senator who voted against the bill; Ada and all but one of the twenty-one senators are Catholic.

March 20, 1990
Washington, DC
Cardinal Joseph Bernardin of Chicago asserts in a talk at Georgetown University's Woodstock Theological Center that "a public figure who is personally opposed to abortion but not publicly opposed ... is an unacceptable fulfillment of a public role." Bernardin insists that public officials have a responsibility to work to enact laws to "protect unborn life."

March 27, 1990
Albany, New York
A news report says that Reverend Anthony Napolitano of St. Ann's Catholic Church in Yonkers has prohibited school children from meeting with state senator Nicholas Spano at the capitol. Because of Spano's adoption of a pro-choice position in January, the priest claims that contact with Spano would be "counterproductive to the school's values and the values of our children."

April 4, 1990
Washington, DC
The NCCB's Committee for Pro-Life Activities announces a new antiabortion campaign. The bishops have a contract with Hill & Knowlton, a Madison Avenue public relations firm, as well as with a polling firm, the Wirthlin Group, to launch a five-year, five-million-dollar media campaign to end legal abortion. The Knights of Columbus have contributed three million dollars toward the campaign.

April 6, 1990
Pennsylvania
Pennsylvania's Catholic bishops issue a pastoral letter on abortion and public policy five weeks before the state primary. Signed by the state's eighteen bishops, it exhorts Catholics as well as "all persons of good will" to stop abortion. It states that Catholics have a "special duty" to oppose abortion and that anyone repudiating church teaching on the issue "cannot claim to be a Catholic in good standing."

May 6, 1990
Providence, Rhode Island
The Roman Catholic Diocese of Providence, Rhode Island, instructs the Prout Memorial High School in South Kingston to cancel a talk by state representative Patrick Kennedy (son of US Senator Edward Kennedy) because the legislator is a Catholic who supports a woman's right to choose abortion. Kennedy was scheduled to speak at a mother-daughter breakfast; abortion was not the subject of the talk.

May 10, 1990
Las Vegas, Nevada
Bishop Daniel Walsh issues a letter, read to Nevada Catholics at Mass, warning that the Catholic church's position on abortion is likely to be misrepresented during the debate over Nevada's impending abortion rights referendum. He writes that Catholic citizens should not endorse the "grave evil" of "abortion on demand."

Two weeks earlier, Walsh refused to allow a Catholic prochoice candidate for attorney general to address a Catholic grade-school government class in his diocese.

May 18, 1990
North Wildwood, New Jersey
During New Jersey's annual Knights of Columbus convention, Bishop James McHugh says, "Any politician who had determinedly and consistently and clearly taken a prochoice stance, that person should not be given an honor or any forum in this diocese." Two weeks later, New Jersey governor Jim Florio resigns from the Knights.

May 23, 1990
Trenton, New Jersey
Bishop John Reiss announces through a diocesan spokesman that prochoice Catholic politicians are barred from speaking at church-sponsored events, receiving honors from the church, or holding church office in his diocese.

June 2, 1990
Peoria, Illinois
Bishop John Myers states in a pastoral letter that it is "immoral for church members to vote for candidates who favor abortion rights" and that prochoice Catholics should refrain from receiving Communion.

June 14, 1990
New York
Cardinal O'Connor writes in his diocesan newspaper that, "for the common good," prochoice Catholic politicians "must be warned that they are at risk of excommunication." When prochoice advocacy "persists, bishops may consider excommunication the only option."

July 2, 1990
Bethesda, Maryland
Monsignor William O'Donnell, pastor of Our Lady of Lourdes parish in Bethesda, tells John Hurson, candidate for the Maryland House of Delegates, that Hurson must resign from the parish council because of his prochoice position. O'Donnell says the fact that "Hurson held a leadership position in the church and had publicized it in campaign leaflets was critical to the decision to remove him from the council." At a widely covered news conference, Hurson refuses to resign.

President Clinton has been making a full-court press for Catholic voters: Pushing for peace in North[ern] Ireland. Extolling Mother Teresa. Talking about values. Even endorsing the school uniforms familiar to generations of parochial school students.

Susan Page, USA Today, April 1996

Unlike the days when there was such a thing as "the Catholic vote" and it was dependably Democratic, today's Catholics are divided evenly among Republican, Democratic, and Independent parties.

Laurie Goodstein, Washington Post, June 1996

American Catholicism in a Pluralistic Society

By Mary C. Segers

Being an American Catholic has never been easy. Our nation's history has been marked by periodic waves of nativism and anti-Catholic hysteria prompted by Protestant suspicions of the loyalty and allegiance of Catholic citizens. From the banning of priests in colonial New York to the burning of a Charlestown, Massachusetts, convent in 1834 to the anti-Catholicism of the Ku Klux Klan in the 1920s, Catholic Americans have been subjected periodically to outbursts of mistrust, suspicion, and contempt.

Protestants wondered whether Catholics could be good American citizens. They worried that Catholics would not take seriously the obligations of citizenship in a democratic republic. At bottom, they questioned whether American Catholics could fully endorse the ideals of disestablishment and free exercise of religion enshrined in the First Amendment to the US Constitution.

Although Protestant fears were largely exaggerated, they were not without foundation. Throughout nineteenth-century European history, the Roman Catholic church evinced little tolerance of liberal democracy with its corollary ideas of church-state separation and religious freedom. Papal statements in the nineteenth century contained outright disavowals of religious freedom. In 1832, Pope Gregory XVI denounced the idea of church-state separation as a "crazed absurdity" (*delirum mentem*). Pope Pius IX referred to religious liberty as "madness" and roundly condemned it in his 1864 *Syllabus of Errors*. Statements like these made non-Catholics nervous.

In his essay "American Catholics and American Society," historian David O'Brien has aptly described Protestant fears of Catholic power: "Like the American of recent times who wondered whether the United States could tolerate the presence of subversives bent on the overthrow of free institutions, Protestants in the nineteenth century wondered whether the experiment in self-government could survive the presence of a massive Catholic population organized under hierarchical control, in separate churches and schools, upholding an intolerant view of religious liberty, making exclusive claims for their denomination, and recognizing the authority of a foreign, supposedly infallible pope, who taught that all the modern liberties, including freedom of conscience and church-state separation, were violations of the law of God. Anti-Catholics were hardly crazy and anti-Catholicism could easily appear as one of those reform movements seeking to insure the success of the American republic."

Mary C. Segers teaches political theory and religion and politics at Rutgers University. She is the editor of Church Polity and American Politics: Issues in Contemporary Catholicism *(1990) and other books. Segers is currently writing a book on religion and politics in the United States entitled* A Wall of Separation? Debating the Role of Religion in Public Life. *This article appeared in* Conscience, Summer 1996.

The Church's Tripartite Survival Strategy

Yet American Catholicism flourished in this democratic republic committed to church-state separation. From a church of predominantly poor immigrants, it developed into the largest single denomination in the United States, now numbering sixty million or 22 percent of the population. Moreover, church leaders skillfully developed a tripartite strategy of affirming American religious arrangements while insuring the possibility of a Catholic presence in American life. First, they distinguished carefully between spiritual and temporal affairs and used this as the basis for defending the pope's spiritual supremacy while strongly denying any papal influence in secular politics. They likewise defined their own leadership as moral and spiritual and strongly insisted that Catholic lay people remained free in political matters. In this way, the bishops followed a policy of nonpartisanship and respect for church-state separation.

Second, the Catholic hierarchy used the American tradition of disestablishment and church-state separation to defend the rights of Catholics. In the name of separation they insisted on their right and duty to defend their church against any effort to impose alien values or to exclude Catholics from public life. This led the bishops to demand the removal, for instance, of Protestant bibles and anti-Catholic texts from schools and to insist upon access for Catholic clergy to prisons and public hospitals. They resisted proposals to nationalize education and fought unsuccessfully in the states for school aid.

Third, the Catholic hierarchy demonstrated public-spiritedness in times of national crisis. The bishops rallied to the nation's cause in the First and Second World Wars and instructed American Catholics in the responsibilities of citizenship. They supported the New Deal during the 1930s, defending unions and government efforts toward social reform. In this way the bishops acted as moral leaders with public responsibilities to educate Catholic citizens and to affirm and strengthen the community and the nation.

The bishops' three-part strategy of detached nonpartisanship, public-spiritedness, and militant defense of group rights received theoretical affirmation in the mid-twentieth century in the work of the Jesuit theologian John Courtney Murray. He argued that constitutional provisions of religious freedom and church-state separation were articles of civil peace, not theological doctrines. As civil arrangements, they left the church free to worship and did not require the church to assent to falsehood or indifferentism. Moreover, Murray contended, Catholicism taught as true those doctrines of human dignity, justice, and freedom that were central to the American tradition of equality and inalienable rights. He thus insisted that far from making Catholics bad citizens, Catholicism provided a tradition of moral reasoning which supported the American tradition of liberal democracy and constitutional rights.

Murray distinguished sharply between spiritual and temporal affairs and pointed to those elements in Catholic jurisprudence affirming a distinction between law and morality. His work made it possible for Catholic bishops such as Cardinal Richard Cushing of Boston to accept the legalization of birth control in the 1960s. In acceding to the reform of the Massachusetts birth control law in 1965, Cushing stated: "It is important to note that Catholics do not need the support of civil law to be faithful to their religious

> American Catholicism flourished in the United States—a democratic republic committed to church-state separation.

convictions, and they do not seek to impose by law their moral views on other members of society." Murray's work signified the arrival of American Catholics as full participants in society much as the election of President John F. Kennedy signaled the end of overt anti-Catholicism in American politics.

No sooner had Murray made the case for being American and Catholic, however, than new elements within the Catholic community arose to challenge the national ethos. During the sixties, the Catholic Left challenged the hierarchy's support of the Vietnam War and insisted that the church forcefully resist racist tendencies within American society. The Second Vatican Council (1962-1965) provided intellectual support for this prophetic, critical role that the American church has freely assumed in the last quarter of the twentieth century.

> Catholics should be vocal in asserting the right and duty of all religious groups in a pluralistic society to address the moral dimensions of public issues.

Vatican II and Change

Indeed, any attempt to understand the church's role in abortion politics since *Roe v. Wade* must begin with analysis of the sea change represented by Vatican II. Here the most important conciliar documents are the *Declaration on Religious Liberty*, which affirmed Murray's arguments for the religious freedom of non-Catholics, and the *Pastoral Constitution on the Church in the Modern World*, which shifted the church away from a defensive position to a more active engagement with the world. While the church has no political agenda of its own, the council fathers taught, it has a responsibility to share in public life and in particular to defend and promote human rights and human dignity. On this basis the bishops have addressed global concerns such as poverty, racism, illiteracy, disease, economic injustice, and war and peace. Every four years, the American hierarchy has issued statements on political responsibility addressing a wide range of problems. The 1983 pastoral letter on war and peace and the 1986 pastoral on economic justice flow directly from this conciliar vision of the church responding to the central issues of human dignity in our time. Obviously, the church sees its role in abortion politics as an outgrowth of this concern with human rights. The present pope, John Paul II, makes this very clear in his 1995 encyclical *Evangelium Vitae*, which calls on Catholics—especially doctors, legislators, and other opinion-leaders—to oppose abortion, euthanasia, assisted suicide, and with some qualifications, capital punishment.

It is useful to summarize the changes Vatican II wrought in the church's attitude towards modernity and the modern world. Prior to the council, the church lived in a defensive ghetto protecting institutional interests and zealously guarding a view of itself as virtually the sole possessor of truth. The standard teaching held that religious liberty was an accommodation to a less than ideal situation in which the rights of non-Catholics had to be tolerated for reasons of expediency. The council's *Declaration on Religious Liberty* changed all that, affirming religious freedom as an intrinsic right rooted in human dignity.

From a non-Catholic perspective, this was a momentous achievement in ecumenical and church-state relations. No longer need American Protestants, Jews, agnostics, or atheists fear that a Catholic majority might deny their right to believe, worship, and practice according to conscience. Pope John XXIII had made the critical distinction in his encyclical *Pacem in Terris* that while error had no rights, the erroneous conscience of the nonbeliever must be respected. Catholics now had a positive duty to respect the sincerely held beliefs and practices of non-Catholics.

At the same time, the council fathers affirmed the right and duty of Catholics to join non-Catholics in common action to meet the needs of the world today. The *Pastoral Constitution on the Church in the Modern World* legitimated the social ministry of the church and became the basis for new forms of political ministry by priests, religious, and laity on behalf of social justice and peace. Lay Catholics in particular were enjoined to use their special expertise to develop public policies enhancing human dignity and human rights. Implicit in conciliar teaching was the notion that all citizens have a responsibility to consider the moral dimensions of issues when deciding among parties and candidates. The moral principles to be considered comprised the catalogue of human rights developed in church teaching since John XXIII's *Pacem in Terris*, including both political and civil rights like free speech, freedom of the press, freedom of religion, and the right and duty of political participation, and social and economic rights necessary for living in dignity.

The Abortion Politics Dilemma

This ambiguous legacy of Vatican II may help to explain the dilemma American Catholics experience in the debate over public policy on abortion. On one hand, Catholics have a moral duty to respect the religious freedom and conscience rights of non-Catholics. On the other hand, Catholics have a responsibility to bring religious and moral principles to bear in the formulation of humane public policies. The case has been made elsewhere that a prochoice position can be compatible with Catholic moral teaching. But for those Catholics who support the bishops' position that abortion can never be a moral choice, the question remains of its legal status, and there Catholics may find themselves in a conflict with the bishops. How may Catholic officeholders and citizens resolve this dilemma?

From the perspective of Catholic lawmakers, several considerations come to mind. First, it is important for Catholic citizens and public officials to defend the rights of religious groups, such as the church, to contribute to public debate, and public policy formation. Periodically throughout the controversy over abortion policy, the old anti-Catholicism has reappeared as editors and commentators have accused Catholic clergy of actions and policies breaching the "wall of separation" between church and state. Catholics should be vocal in asserting the right and duty of all religious groups in a pluralistic society to address the moral dimensions of public issues. Religious freedom hardly means that religion is to be privatized or that believers can talk only to each other.

At the same time, churches are not merely pressure groups defending their own particular interests in the policy process. While churches may lobby legislators and testify before congressional committees, they also have a special responsibility to attend to the common good and to universal values of peace and justice. In a religiously diverse society, they should conduct themselves in ways that do not incite sectarian strife. Thus, if churchmen wish to press vigorously a particular policy position (such as protection of fetal life), prudence requires that they calculate carefully the consequences of their political strategies and policy recommendations.

Second, Catholic politicians may point to the American bishops' pastoral letters on economic justice and on war and peace as examples illustrating how

Pope John Paul II caricatures democracy as a majoritarian tyranny.

Catholics may usefully contribute to public debate. In these two cases the bishops, recognizing their lack of competence in policy matters, consulted experts and scholars—Catholic and non-Catholic, supporters and dissenters. The bishops also distinguished between general moral principles and particular public policies, acknowledging that prudent application of moral norms to particular social conditions might result in policies different from those the bishops recommended. Moreover, the tone of both these letters was respectful towards those (non-Catholic and Catholic) in disagreement with the bishops.

Unfortunately, the bishops have adopted none of these precautions in the matter of abortion policy. There has been little consultation with professionals such as demographers and medical experts, certainly not with anyone who might be called "prochoice." With the single exception of Archbishop Rembert Weakland of Milwaukee, the hierarchy has not consulted women who disagree with the church's policy recommendations. The bishops have made no distinction between moral norms and policy applications, arguing instead that the moral teaching against abortion must be fully reflected in civil law. Finally, while the bishops never penalized Catholic politicians who differed from their policy recommendations on nuclear war or economic justice, they have specifically targeted Catholic lawmakers who disagreed with their policy position on abortion. In recent years, threats to public officials of excommunication, warnings of eternal perdition, denial of communion, and exclusion from parish ministry have regrettably become commonplace. With the publication in 1995 of Pope John Paul II's encyclical *Evangelium Vitae* (*The Gospel of Life*), the pressure on Catholic legislators has become even more intense.

In his encyclical, the pope characterizes laws permitting abortion or euthanasia as intrinsically unjust and without legal validity or binding force. He says Catholic citizens should oppose and resist such laws through peaceful conscientious objection. He also states that it is impermissible for Catholic public officials to take part in a propaganda campaign in favor of such laws, or to vote for such laws.

In countries which already have legalized abortion, the pope suggests that lawmakers may support compromise measures limiting but not banning abortions. The reasoning here is that such compromise measures do "not in fact represent an illicit cooperation with an unjust law, but rather a legitimate and proper attempt to limit its evil aspects" (§73).

The pope's refusal to accept legalized abortion stems from his conception of democracy and from his understanding of Catholic tradition on the relationship of law and morality. John Paul II chastises democracies for denying the fundamental inalienable right to life on the basis of the will of the majority. And he draws upon Aquinas's jurisprudential writings to emphasize that a valid law cannot, in principle, command or permit a gravely immoral action.

Unfortunately, the pope caricatures democracy as a majoritarian tyranny, thereby indicating that he simply does not understand liberal democracy with its emphasis upon individual and minority rights as well as majority rule. Moreover, the pope fails to see that the real challenge in many democratic societies is their religious pluralism. Advanced, complex democracies must take into account such diversity and may have to pass laws permitting abortion in deference to the diverse religious and conscientious judgments of the citizenry. The editors of

> With the publication of *Evangelium Vitae*, the pressure on Catholic legislators has become even more intense.

Commonweal summarize succinctly the deficiencies of the papal criticism of democracy:

> *The pope's rhetoric and style do not fully acknowledge the complexity of the political situation. Individual rights and personal autonomy are the philosophical bedrock of Western society.... Judging modern democracy uniquely depraved is neither plausible nor persuasive.*

Finally, the pope is selective in his interpretation of Aquinas's famous passages on law and morality. He quotes Aquinas to the effect that an unjust law is no law at all, but he then ignores St. Thomas's cautionary warning that citizens should be careful about disobeying unjust laws, less they give scandal and contribute to public disorder. Apparently, John Paul II is not impressed with the realism of Catholic political and legal thought about the proper relation between law and morals. After all, the church has traditionally recognized that, while law and morality are related, they are not coterminous. There are limits to the law as a method of social control, as Aquinas argued. Lawmakers must consider whether measures they enact will be acceptable and evoke compliance, and whether they will achieve their intended effect or result in a situation far worse than the original problem the law was supposed to remedy. These questions of sound lawmaking assume far greater significance in a pluralistic, religiously diverse society, such as the United States, which is committed to religious freedom and church-state separation. In such a society, the church's conception of the pedagogical function of the law—that the law is a moral teacher—is difficult to sustain on controverted issues where there is little consensus.

Responses for Catholic Legislators

Faced with such pressures from clergy and hierarchy, how may Catholic legislators respond? First, they must remind the church that, in a pluralistic democracy, lawmakers have obligations to conscience, constituents, the Constitution, and the common good. When these duties conflict, there are no simple, automatic solutions to the question of appropriate public policy. Instead, lawmakers have a duty to seek policy outcomes that balance the above-mentioned competing claims.

Second, Catholic lawmakers must educate church officials to the realities of policy making in a pluralistic society constitutionally committed to religious freedom and to church-state separation. They must demonstrate to the bishops that a politician who supports legalized abortion despite personal moral opposition is embracing a perfectly respectable, morally defensible policy position. In a pluralistic society, not every religious belief or religiously-derived conviction can or should be converted into public law. Both American legal tradition and Catholic jurisprudence recognize a distinction between law and morals. Moreover, as former New York Governor Mario Cuomo has argued, in a democratic society, values derived from faith traditions "will not—and should not—be accepted as part of the public morality unless they are shared by the pluralistic community at large, by consensus." In democratic policy making, consensus is crucial, and consensus is the result of persuasion, not coercion. Religious and political leaders may try to shape a policy consensus, but in the end public acceptability of the wisdom of a particular proposal is decisive.

Third, Catholic politicians can remind their bishops that in a liberal democracy, not even consensus is controlling, because

> The bishops have made no distinction between moral norms and policy applications.

> "Catholics do not need the support of civil law to be faithful to their religious convictions," Cardinal Cushing said.

prudent policy making always looks to the consequences of laws enacted. A public officeholder has a moral duty to estimate, as best she can, the consequences of reinstating restrictive abortion laws. Policy makers must calculate the *efficacy* of restrictive laws (whether citizens will comply with them), the *enforceability* of such laws (whether police will enforce them selectively, uniformly, or not at all), and the *effects* of such laws (whether, on balance, the negative effects of reinstating restrictive laws will outweigh the positive benefits). It is the special province of lawmakers to make prudential judgments about the probable results of proposed policies. Thus, even if a popular consensus develops in favor of restrictive abortion laws, a public officeholder is still obliged to judge whether the proposed policy will make sound law. The 1990 veto of a highly restrictive antiabortion statute by Idaho's Governor Cecil Andrus (whose personal beliefs are antiabortion) pointedly illustrates this political duty of lawmakers.

In sum, the responsibilities of Catholic policy makers in a pluralistic democracy are complex and cannot be distilled into a simplistic duty to enact church teaching into civil law. By calling attention to the many factors and duties which are part of a politician's vocation, Catholic legislators may remind their bishops of the legitimate autonomy of secular politics and of the special expertise and responsibilities of policy making. Humility and prudence require that bishops respect the competency of lay Catholic lawmakers.

The principled position of prochoice Catholic lawmakers reflects a commitment to exercise prudence in making sound public policy. It also embodies a commitment to protect the religious freedom of constituents who do not share the antiabortion views of the Roman Catholic hierarchy. It begs the question to say, as the bishops insist, that abortion is a moral rather than a religious issue about which all citizens can come to some rational consensus. The plain fact is that religious groups disagree fundamentally on the morality of abortion. Some traditions maintain that abortion is immoral, others hold that abortion may be the lesser of two evils, while still others contend that moral duties of responsible parenthood may permit and even demand abortion in many circumstances. Moreover, the same fundamental disagreement about the morality of abortion exists among secular philosophers. Catholic teaching may hold that the wrongness of abortion is a matter of moral reasoning based upon principles of natural law that are accessible to all human beings, not just to Catholics. However, lack of consensus indicates that few have found natural law arguments about abortion to be persuasive.

When those who define the moral standards of a free society cannot agree, there is little warrant for passage of coercive or restrictive legislation. However, there may be considerable justification for enacting social policies (prenatal care, maternal and child health care, sex education, day care, and housing) which get at the root causes of abortion. Such policies can help to reduce the incidence of abortion without coercing women.

The church can learn from Catholic officeholders the need to exercise prudence and caution in attempting to shape abortion policy. By acting to preserve the rights of all citizens as well as the legitimate autonomy of government in a liberal democracy, Catholic lawmakers will be performing an invaluable service to the republic—just as Catholic clergy can serve the nation well by challenging American citizens to examine carefully the many values at stake in the abortion dilemma. ⊕

Political Activity and Tax-Exempt Status

One condition of the tax-exempt status held by most churches—under section 501(c)(3) of the Internal Revenue Code—is that 501(c)(3) organizations cannot engage in any electoral campaign activity, and lobbying cannot constitute a "substantial" portion of their work. Every four years, the general counsel of the United States Catholic Conference issues a memo to guide dioceses and churches on which political activities are permissible and which are not under the church's tax-exemption. Excerpts of the guidelines issued in February 1996 follow.

Permitted Activities

During election campaigns, Catholic organizations may educate voters about the issues. In addition, they may educate voters about candidates' positions on the issues, through presentation of candidate forums and distribution of voter education materials, including incumbents' voting records, results of candidate polls or questionnaires, and candidates' statements. Such activities, if unbiased, will not violate the political campaign activity prohibition. Although the code does not define bias, activities or publications generally would be considered biased if they indicate or imply (1) that a candidate agrees or disagrees with the organization's position, or (2) that an organization agrees or disagrees with the candidate's position. Whether an activity or publication is biased depends on all the facts and circumstances, including format, content, and manner of conduct or publication. All voter education publications should include a statement of their educational purpose and a disclaimer of any intent to endorse or oppose any candidate or political party.

Caveat: You should be wary of outside groups seeking permission to distribute their educational materials through Catholic organizations.... The organizations preparing these voter education materials may not be Section 501(c)(3) organizations, and thus may not even be subject to its political activity prohibition. The fact that it may be permissible for them to distribute their voter guides does not make it appropriate for Catholic organizations to do so....

IRS has concluded that distribution during the election campaign of a biased voting record, i.e., one that indicated the organization's position and whether the legislator voted in accordance with that position, can avoid the political campaign activity prohibition only in extremely limited circumstances. The criteria set by IRS are: (1) the voting record must not identify candidates for re-election; (2) distribution must not be timed to coincide with any election, but rather must be one of a series of regularly distributed voting records; (3) distribution must not be targeted to areas where elections are occurring; and (4) the voting record must not be broadly disseminated to the electorate, but rather to a limited group, such as to members of the organization or subscribers to its publication....

Prohibited Activities

Catholic organizations may not make statements, either oral or written, supporting or opposing any candidate for elective public office, any slate of candidates, political party, or political action committee. This would include statements made in a sermon, a church bulletin, or an editorial in a Catholic periodical, and distribution of filled-in sample ballots. In addition, Catholic organizations should avoid statements that indirectly support or oppose a particular candidate, e.g., labeling a candidate as prolife or antifamily, using plus (+) or minus (-) or similar signs that indicate candidates' agreement (or lack thereof) with the organizations' positions on issues....

A Catholic organization may not provide financial support to any candidate, PAC, or political party. Likewise, it may not provide or solicit in-kind support, such as free or selective use of volunteers, paid staff, facilities, equipment, mailing lists, etc. Further, a Catholic organization may not solicit financial support for or in opposition to any candidate, PAC, or political party, e.g., by taking a collection or passing the basket at an organizational activity, or by using the organization's letterhead to solicit contributions....

A Catholic organization should not distribute or authorize distribution of campaign literature, biased voter education material, etc., through member mailings, during worship services, or by other means, whether by its own employees or representatives or by the representatives of a candidate, political party, or PAC. Since religious organizations lack authority to control access to public property, e.g., public streets and sidewalks, third-party distribution of partisan materials on adjacent public property should not be imputed to a Catholic organization.

Parking lots deserve special attention, since automobile windshields seem to present irresistible targets for leafleting. Although certain cases related to leafleting in shopping malls and their parking lots ... may cause some to argue otherwise, the parking lots of Catholic organizations generally should be considered private property.

[Catholics] are not necessarily voting on moral issues. They vote their self-interest. They want to control taxes, spending, and crime, but they are still sensitive to stepping on the little guy.

Tony Fabrizio, pollster for the Dole campaign, February 1996